THE **UNLEASHED** LIFE

DISCOVER YOUR INNER POWER

THE UNLEASHED LIFE

DISCOVER YOUR INNER POWER

THE UNLEASHED LIFE.
Discover Your Inner Power.

©2024 Marek Mularczyk

All rights reserved. No portion of this book may be reproduced, stored, or transmitted in any form - electronic, photocopying, scanning, or other - except for brief quotations in reviews or articles, without the prior written permission of the author.

ISBN 978-0-9571214-9-2 (print)
ISBN 978-1-3999-8644-1 (ePub)

Cover and book design:
Marek Mularczyk
www.marekmularczyk.com

*This book is dedicated to you
and the angel inside of you.
I hope you find your true purpose in life
and set your angel free.*

" Never, never, never give up "

*" When you arise in the morning,
think of what a precious privilege
it is to be alive
- to breathe, to think,
to enjoy, to love. "*

Introduction

Welcome. I am here to tell you that you are an important person. You are a much more important person than you think you are. And you are here for a reason. I want you to know that you are loved by God (or any higher power you believe in). I am here to remind you of that and to support you in your journey to discover your real self. You are a divine, spiritual being living on a physical plane. YOU have created everything in your life. YOU are a real creator. YOU have the power to create any reality you desire. And I want to help you to start believing in yourself.

There may have been many teachers in your past who appeared in your life and tried to remind you of your greatness and my guess is, you may have dismissed them and their teachings. Some of you may even have ended up worshipping them and making them your "gurus". This book is not about me, it is about YOU. It is time for you to realise your self-worth and your divinity. It is time for you to realise your infinite potential. It is time for you to find your inner power.

You are a special person and you are going to hear that from me many times in this book. You may not think that, you may not think that our world needs you, but the truth is that the world does need you. Why, you may ask? Because you are a unique being that appeared on the surface of our planet. No one like you has ever been here before and no one like you will ever appear here again. No one has exactly the same voice as you and no one can smile exactly the same as you. No one can take your place as it is yours and you, not anybody else, need to fill it here on the Earth.

> *"You are a beautiful human being,*
> *no matter how old you are*
> *or how young you are,*
> *whether you're white or black,*
> *tall or short, wealthy or poor*
> *you are an image of God."*
>
> Marek Mularczyk

When you arrive here on our planet, you do not arrive with any special plan. You are not given, or should not be given, any directives on what your life should be like and what you should do. There is only one plan for you that God has for you - to be joyful, to live a life full of joy. The more joyful you are in everything you are doing, the closer you are to your divinity. Being joyful in what you do is one of the greatest accomplishments in life. You possess a great power, a power to create anything you desire. And you can feel great anytime you want, you can direct your feelings in the right direction to fullfill your destiny.

But it's not always like that. It's not always good times. Bad times come as well. And it's the hard times that teach you most. Time of challenges. Time of hardship. Hard times will stay inside you, inside your heart, inside your soul. Hard times will make you stronger if only you persist and never give up in this journey called life.

And unfortunately, we don't learn at school how to deal with hard times. We don't learn at school how to deal with challenges in life, how to handle them. Your ability to handle challenges in your life is a measure of your character. But school doesn't teach that. School teaches how to read and write, and how to do mathematical calculations, and we need that. But what you don't learn at school is how to deal with life's challenges. How do you handle a loss of a loved one? How do you handle a loss of a job? How do you handle rejection? This explains why so many people in these situations feel lost and don't know what to do. How are they supposed to know that if nobody taught them? This explains why so many people in these situations not knowing how to handle them turn to alcohol or drugs. They're not bad people. They're just lost. They lost direction. They lost the sight of the shore in this ocean we call life.

But I'm here to tell you that no matter what happens to you in life, there is always a reason to keep going. Never give up. There is always a way. My goal here is to inspire you to look beyond the challenges that happen to you and keep going in the direction of your goals or dreams. I believe in you. I believe you can do it. And just so you know, you deserve to enjoy your life.

> *"Whatever you can do, or dream you can, begin it.*
> *Boldness has genius, power and magic in it. "*

*" Someone once told me
the definition of hell:
the last day you have on earth,
the person you became
will meet the person
you could have become "*

anonymous

A New Chapter in Life

*"Live as if you were to die tomorrow,
learn as if you were to live forever. "*

Do you know what your life's purpose is? Sadly most people don't. Your life's purpose is not your job, you are not your job. Your life's purpose is something bigger than that. You are meant to live a meaningful life. You are meant to find a true purpose in your life. Finding your purpose in life will make you a happier person. If you have found your purpose then you know what I'm talking about.

So many people are stuck in their meaningless jobs and are working Monday to Friday waiting for the weekend to come. I remember hearing one day on the radio, when a speaker on the radio (this was a Wednesday) at some point announced with excitement "We made it! It's Wednesday! We're half-way through the working week! Only two more days to go and then weekend!"

Can you imagine waiting for the weekend every waking hour of your every weekday. Can you imagine living just two days out of seven?! What a disgusting way to live. These people are always waiting until Saturday arrives. This is so sad. Why not live every single day to the fullest?

I work with a lot of people from all different walks of life and you know what I hear most, especially near the end of the week? " Thank goodness, it's Friday." But what about the rest of your week? If you only are happy two days out of seven, then you only live 28% of your life! What about the other 72% of your life, which is a majority of your live? If you're stuck in a job you don't like, it is time to do something about it.

I know what it feels like. I've been there. I worked in a place that I used to like working, but as I evolved and increased my competency in my field, I noticed that I could do better, I could do more. I knew I didn't want to stay in that job anymore. And probably like yourself, I didn't know what to do. But I also knew that it was time to do something, anything. And I hear that very often from people around me, people saying "I don't like my job, but I don't know what to do." And I understand that. The sad truth, however, is that everyone knows what they want to do or could know if they gave it some time, but people are too busy with their "busy life" to stop and take time to think through what they want to do with their lives.

Back to my story, I knew I didn't want to work in that place anymore. I knew I grew up emotionally and professionally and I was too good for the job and I wanted to do something meaningful in life. I wanted to make a difference in people's lives. I didn't know exactly what I wanted to do, but I knew that I didn't want to stay there.

So I quit my job! And I gave myself one month to work it out (I had one month notice).

This was a very scary perspective, not to mention that I was in a foreign country, far away from my family, and didn't have any "contacts" and didn't know many people, but I knew I had to push myself off the edge. I needed a push to get me in the open and challenge myself to find out what I wanted to do in life and start doing it.

And in just a few days' time I knew what I wanted to do! It wasn't easy but it was worth it. It felt so good to say "I'm leaving." This was a turning point in my life. And this was just a start. A start of a new chapter in life. A new journey. And I invite you to take this new journey through life with me, to begin a new chapter in your life.

Don't just work on your job to pay your bills. Don't just work on your job because you feel like you have no freedom to do whatever you like. Find something that makes you jump out of the bed every morning with joy and happiness. And if you haven't found it yet, keep looking! And in the meantime, find purpose in what you are doing as it brings you closer to your goal.

How do you find it? First of all, stop and give it some thought. Spend some quality time with yourself exploring possibilities. Ask yourself some questions:

- What do you love doing?
- What makes you happy?
- What is really important to you?

Find something that would keep you awake long into the night and wake you up in the morning. Like myself writing this right now. It's late at night, everyone's asleep. It's quiet on the streets, just occasional cars on the roads.

If you know me, you will hear me saying things like "It's Monday again!" with a smile on my face.

Now it is time for you to explore what you want to do with your life. How do you start? Start by asking yourself what is the most important to you in your life? What do you love doing? What could you be doing all day long without checking the time all the time? Find where your passion is. Explore your inner self. Give yourself some time on your own to discover your purpose in life. Most of the time we are so busy with 'doing things' that we don't give ourselves time to stop and think.

Wouldn't it be incredible if you could touch other people's lives? Wouldn't it be incredible if you could leave legacy so people would remember you long after you're gone? What legacy would you like to leave? How would you want people to remember you? We live in an era where we don't connect with other people as much as we used to in the past. We have created amazing technologies and we can measure with a precision of a fraction of a second the timing of exploding bombs or landing on another planet, but we have difficulties in connecting with our friends and neighbours.

As sad as it is, I think Deepak Chopra put it in great context when saying that:

" We live in a high-tech low-touch society. "

Take a moment and ponder on what you could do to make your life more meaningful. How could you make a difference in the world? And don't think you couldn't because you could. Each of us has something that can share with the world.

And please don't wait too long because soon your life will be over. Don't wait till tomorrow, the day after tomorrow or for a better day.

As someone once said:

"There is no tomorrow, there is only today. "

I love what George Bernard Shaw said, when on his deathbed he was asked what he would do differently if he could live his life again. He said:

*"I'd like to be the person
I could have been but never was. "*

Beautiful and so deep.

Please be a person you could be. Become this person now.

Pursuit of Happiness

*"The ultimate aim of human life
is to be happy. "*

How to get what you want in life? Why is it that some people have everything and others struggle all the time? Why is it that not everyone can enjoy prosperity and fulfilled life?

Many of us search for happiness in life. We buy new "personal development" books. We attend more and more seminars. We buy all these books hoping they hold the secret to life of happiness. Life of abundance. Yet we don't find the answer. And we buy another book and another one and another one. Why do we keep buying them? Maybe it's because we're thinking that the last book got us very close to the answer but it wasn't the right one? And it's not just books. It could be relationship or a teacher.

Those of us who are persistent and searching for solutions to daily problems reach out everywhere. But why is it that so many of us are still looking? What are we looking for? Are we looking for something that is within reach? Isn't what we're looking for in our lives already? Maybe we're just not noticing it but it's already there?

Why is it that even though we have this amazing technology, where we can send people to the moon and create these amazing devices and yet so many of us are unhappy and so many are starving? It doesn't make any sense, does it?

Is it because for so long we have been told that we cannot control our lives and our circumstances? That's what people have believed for generations. And that's what many of us still believe today. That's why so many of us struggle all their lives. Trying to meet demands of living.

We came to live on our beautiful planet to feel good. When we feel good, when we have good feelings, we are moving towards something that we wanted for a long time. We are moving towards something that will make us happy. Something that will make our lives better. And yet, at the same time, we drift away from our "pursuit of happiness", we're drifting into the ocean we call life and away from the shore where our destiny awaits.

> *"One day*
> *you'll look back on this moment*
> *and you'll be so glad*
> *you didn't give up on yourself. "*

Change Your Life

*"When we least expect it,
life sets us a challenge
to test our courage
and willingness to change."*

Bad things happen. Life is not just about good things happening. And when bad things happen, you need to believe that good things will follow and will raise you even higher than you were to help you reach your goal and your special mission in life.

When it comes to changing your life, it may seem like it's going to take a long time before you see any changes. You may feel like it's not even worth it to waste all your energy and that's where so many people quit even before they start.

Please, don't be a quitter. Be a fighter. Be a survivor. Fight for your life.

All you need to start improving your life is to start doing something, anything. Start changing your life. Do something you haven't done before. And it doesn't have to be big things. Start small. Do something differently. Get out of your comfort zone.

> *Start small, and keep going.*
> *As you gain more confidence in yourself,*
> *as you gain momentum, keep going!*
> *Don't ever stop!*
>
> Marek Mularczyk

And don't let anyone stop you. Become unstoppable. Don't let anyone ever tell you that you can't do something. Don't let anyone ever tell you that you will not accomplish your goals. Unfortunately so many people do. So many people don't live up to their potential because someone told them that they couldn't do something or that they were "stupid" or not educated enough.

Do you know this story about the eagle? If you don't, let me tell you this powerful story.

A long time ago in a remote valley, there lived a farmer. One day he got tired of the daily routine of running the farm and decided to climb the cliffs that brooded above the valley to see what lay beyond.

He climbed all day until he reached a ledge just below the top of the cliff; there, to his amazement was a nest, full of eggs.

Immediately he knew they were eagle's eggs and he carefully took one and stowed it in his pack; then seeing the sun was low in the sky, he realized it was too late in the day to make the top and slowly began to make his way down the cliff to his farm.

When he got home he put the egg in with the few chickens he kept in the yard. The mother hen was the proudest chicken you ever saw, sitting atop this magnificent egg; and the cockerel couldn't have been prouder.

Sure enough, some weeks later, from the egg emerged a fine, healthy egret. And as is in the gentle nature of chickens, they didn't balk at the stranger in their midst and raised the majestic bird as one of their own.

So it was that the eagle grew up with its brother and sister chicks. It learned to do all the things chickens do: it clucked and cackled, scratching in the dirt for grits and worms, flapping its wings furiously, flying just a few feet in the air before crashing down to earth in a pile of dust and feathers.

It believed resolutely and absolutely it was a chicken.

One day, late in its life, the eagle-who-thought-he-was-a-chicken happened to look up at the sky. High overhead, soaring majestically and effortlessly with scarcely a single beat of its powerful golden wings, was an eagle!

"What's that?!", cried the old eagle in awe. "It's magnificent! So much power and grace! It's beautiful!"

"That's an eagle", replied a nearby chicken, "That's the King of the Birds. It's a bird of the air... not for the likes of us. We're only chickens, we're birds of the earth".

With that, they all cast their eyes downwards once more and continued digging in the dirt.

And so it was that the eagle lived and died a chicken... because that's all it believed itself to be.

Don't be like this eagle who believed to be a chicken. You are a real eagle and you can spread your wings and fly, high in the sky. You could be this majestic and powerful eagle! You can achieve great things in life. Don't allow anyone to belittle you in pursuit of your dreams.

Here are some ideas for you:
- get up earlier than usual
- take a different route to work/school
- do something you wanted to do for so long but you've been postponing it
- say something nice to someone you meet today

The reasoning behind these ideas is to get you out of your comfort zone. You may feel comfortable in your life but your comfort might be in the way of your personal development.

Start making changes in your life starting from today and notice how your life changes. You will be surprised how small changes in your life may make big impact on the world around you. And this will give you encouragement to make bigger changes in your life.

Here's another idea for you. What would your day look like if you were telling the truth all the time? Ponder over it for a moment. Most of us do seem to lie about something every now and then. Sometimes we don't even realise it. Sometimes we do it not to harm someone else's feelings. However, what we're really doing is not being truthful with ourselves. Sometimes we place responsibility for our happiness on someone else's choice. When we lie, we are not taking responsibility for our own actions. We are not taking responsibility for the consequences of our own actions.

To change your life, you need to stop that. You need to take charge of your life and all the consequences of your decisions. This will give you an opportunity to learn about yourself and the way you think. Be true to yourself. Be true to others. This is your new way of living.

This is the start of your new life.

Be an optimist.

*"Each of us has the choice
each of us owns the power
each of us chooses how to live our lives. "*

Many people say that when you change the way you look at things, your life changes. And that's true. If you're thinking about bad things that could happen, sooner or later something bad will happen. You will notice all the problems and all bad things around you. And as you keep noticing more and more bad things, you will stop trying as you will see no reason to keep trying.

But don't forget about all these good things that happen around you. Try being an optimist. Try it for just one day and your life will change. Challenge yourself to become an optimist and you will see how this will create another perspective on things in your life. I challenge you to become an optimist just for one day. This may be a real life changing experience for you.

Optimists see opportunities everywhere when pessimists see problems. Optimists see opportunities to grow and learn. Instead of getting upset about every single thing, they try to find positives in all circumstances. Optimism is something everyone can learn.

But it takes practice. When you start feeling that something is wrong as you go with your day, try to change it by thinking some positive thoughts. As an optimist try to find something good in everything. Allow your life to be wonderful. Maybe your life is wonderful already but you just didn't look for the good in your life.

Make mistakes.

> *"A life spent making mistakes*
> *is not only more honourable*
> *but more useful than a life*
> *spent doing nothing. "*

So often we are being programmed to think that we can't make mistakes, that we have to be perfect in everything we do. No one is perfect. We are perfectly imperfect. Beautifully imperfect. Everybody makes mistakes although some people may seem to be perfect. Perfection is a burden we place on ourselves.

We all make mistakes as we follow our dreams. Give yourself permission to make mistakes from time to time. It is ok to make mistakes. Relieve yourself of being perfect. Nobody is perfect. Stop being perfect and start following your dreams. Start taking steps towards the changes you always wanted to make. In the past you may have been held back by the fear that you could go wrong or not reach your goal but being wrong is ok. You need to make mistakes every now and then, that's how you learn. You make a mistake, learn from it and move on. Don't let your fears stop you. Think how much better you are going to feel once you know that it's ok to make mistakes and that people are not really watching you or waiting for you to fail. It's just you doing it to yourself. Allow yourself to fail once in a while.

Treat it as a lesson in changing your life and at the same time learning from your mistakes. Try to look at your mistakes as lessons and experiences. When you make a mistake, think about what happened and try to think what you can do in the future to avoid making the same mistake. It's all about learning how to do things better. You will make mistakes as you move towards your better life, but when mistakes happen recognise that it's not a bad thing and start moving past your mistakes quickly and keep moving on.

Find a Hobby

*"To be really happy and really safe,
one ought to have
at least two or three hobbies,
and they must all be real. "*

Do you remember when you were a child and how you had all these hobbies? Do you remember how when you got into doing something you could do it for hours straight? Do you remember how good you were at it? And you just wanted to do it because it made you happy.

Sometimes when negative thoughts start creeping into your mind, you will want to find a way to distract yourself from thinking these thoughts. That's when picking up a hobby will help as your hobby will fill your mind whenever you are feeling not motivated to change your thoughts to positive ones.

There are plenty of things you can do. They can help you to focus your mind on something else instead of focusing on negative thoughts. Some experts often say that when you are trying to break a habit, you need something like a new habit to fill time with something else.

Thank Someone

"Kindness is a language which the deaf can hear and the blind can see."

When you go through changes in your life you may forget about people who stand by you and support you. Don't take their support for granted. Thank the people that help you and stand by you. Thank them for their support. Thank them for their understanding. As you thank them for all their support, you will get their support for your changes that are to come.

Support is something we all need. Even when you focus on changing your life and you do most of the work yourself, you need support. Especially as there will be moments when you will need someone to help you by approaching things differently or changing your perspective. At the moments of changes you will need all the support you can get. And when you get support from others, thank them for their help. It doesn't take much time or effort and it makes other people feel well. They will also be more willing to help you in the future.

We all feel frightened about the future and change. It's moving away from "the old" and to "the new", often unknown new, something unfamiliar. Moving away from things that worked in the past to things that may or may not work. Change doesn't have to be drastic. You can start with small changes to make the process easier for you. Change may be something as simple as doing something you have been doing for a very long time differently than you used to do it. It may be something as simple as picking up a book on something new you would like to learn. By doing small changes you can find the strength for making bigger changes.

If you need help making a change, ask for help. Some people are going to be happy to help you. They enjoy helping others. It brings them happiness, and at the same time this may bring you happiness.

And remember to thank them for their help. Express your gratitude.

Your Health

*"Take care of your body.
It's the only place
you have to live in. "*

Your health is an important part of your life and you should pay close attention to your health. Without good health, everything else becomes less important. Material things become less important. Let me give you an example.

Let's say, you came to money, and now you can afford anything you want, anything you ever wanted. You buy this big house in an affluent area that you always dreamt of. You buy this expensive car you always wanted to drive. You buy all expensive designer clothes you ever wanted. You don't have to work another day in your life. You got all you always dreamt of, everything you always thought would bring you happiness.

And then, one day, you become sick. You go to the doctor and you're told that you have an incurable disease and only have months to live.

You see, without health, even if you get all material possessions in the world, you won't be able to enjoy them. Without good health, nothing else matters.

There are numerous stories of people who spent lives chasing fame and/or money, and once they accumulated all this wealth, as they became sick, they were willing to give all the money away to get their health back but it was too late...

So take good care of your health, take good care of your body.

In a nutshell, you health is all about healthy eating and exercising.

Challenges

> *"One of the greatest challenges in life*
> *is being yourself in a world*
> *that's trying to make you*
> *like anyone else."*
>
> unknown

Life is full of challenges. Life is full of surprises. There will be times in your life when you will be tried, when life will throw something unexpected at you. These things happen. And it's up to you whether you take it as something terrible that happens to you or as a challenge. You have a choice to decide what the situation will mean to you.

If bad things happen to you, think about W Mitchell.

Here's a man who one day had a motorcycle accident that left him with over sixty percent of his body burned. Most of his skin was practically gone. He had no fingers and he spent many months in the hospital bed. He had every reason to want to die. And you know what? He didn't. He didn't give up.

In his own words:

" I could see it as a catastrophe, or as a challenge. I chose the latter. "

It's not just about what happens to you in your life. It's about your reaction to what happens to you. You are the one interpreting the situations to yourself. You are the one to decide what to do with a given situation. When the worst happens you need to keep an eye on your goals and do whatever it takes to stay positive. Look for a way to move forward.

So often so many of us give up too early. This is one of our biggest challenges. To achieve your dream you must never stop. You need to become unstoppable. You need to devote yourself to what you're trying to achieve, whatever it is that represents your dream. You have got to try everything and I believe you will achieve your goal.

Many people who claim that they tried and it wasn't working are often the ones who weren't willing to do whatever it takes. Many people look for excuses to explain why something couldn't be achieved. They're "quitters". They quit as soon as it gets tough.

When things get tough and when you're under pressure and want to quit, I'd like you to remember a speech by Theodore Roosevelt, which he had given at the Sorbonne in Paris in 1910:

It is not the critic that counts;
not the man who points out how the strong man stumbles,
or where the doer of deeds could have done them better.
The credit belongs to the man who is actually in the arena,
whose face is marred by dust and sweat and blood,
who strives valiantly, who errs
and comes up short again and again,
because there is no effort without error or shortcomings,
but who knows the great enthusiasms,
the great devotions;
who spends himself in a worthy cause;
who, at the best, knows, in the end,
the triumph of high achievement,
and who, at the worst, if he fails,
at least he fails while daring greatly,
so that his place shall never be
with those cold and timid souls who knew
neither victory nor defeat.
You've never lived until you've almost died.
For those who have fought for it,
life has a flavour the protected shall never know.

Success

> *"To laugh often and much;*
> *to win the respect of intelligent people*
> *and the affection of children;*
> *to earn the appreciation of honest critics*
> *and endure the betrayal of false friends;*
> *to appreciate beauty;*
> *to find the best in others;*
> *to leave the world a bit better;*
> *whether by a healthy child, a garden patch*
> *or a redeemed social condition;*
> *to know even one life has breathed easier*
> *because you have lived.*
> *This is to have succeeded."*

We all have different ideas about what success is. We all have different dreams in life. Success is not about how much you own and what you have. Success is an ongoing process trying to be more, trying to be a better person. Success, personal success is not an end, it's the road leading to achieve a goal, a dream. It's a way of life. It's about changing your life for better. Emotionally, physically, financially, and more. The power to transform your life lies within you. It's time you took a step to achieve a success you always dreamed of.

To me, every single day being alive is a success. Getting through every single day is a success. Helping another human being is a success. What does a success mean to you?

So how is it that we're not all successful? It's two key elements that are both linked to achieving success: knowledge and action. Yes, anyone can gain knowledge. And knowledge is important. But knowledge on its own will not give you success in life. You need to take action. Action produces results, not knowledge.

If you want to achieve success in life, any success, you need to understand that your internal dialogue is very important to your success. You are not what happens to you. You are in charge of your own feelings and you decide how you want to interpret what happens to you, as I said earlier in this book.

What do you need to achieve success? Just knowledge and take action? No, not just that. You need passion.

Wins And Failures

*" Failure should be our teacher, not our undertaker.
Failure is delay, not defeat.
It is a temporary detour,
not a dead-end.
Failure is something we can avoid
only by saying nothing,
doing nothing, and being nothing. "*

It happens to all of us. We all fail from time to time. But the winners are those who stand up and move on. It's not how many times you failed in the past. It's when you succeed that counts. All winners have failed many times in their past. The stories of the greatest are full of stories of them failing over and over. If you're going through tough times in your life, my advice to you is to 'stick around and give it another try and another one and another one...'. You never know when you may succeed. It may be next time you try. If you don't try, you will never know.

Stories of 'Famous Failures'

There are so many amazing and life-changing success stories of people who never gave up on their dreams. There are so many of them but I just want to share a few of them with you.

Here are some of the stories that inspired me and keep inspiring me every single day.

Did you know that Thomas Edison failed more than 1,000 times when working on a light bulb?

There is a famous story of a journalist coming to Edison and asking him what it feels like to try and fail over 1,000 times. To that Edison replied that he didn't fail over 1,000 times. Instead he proved 1,000 ways in which a light bulb couldn't be invented.

What an amazing story and amazing perspective Edison took when looking at his work.

Did you know that Clint Eastwood was told by an executive at Universal Pictures to forget about being an actor because he talked too slowly and because his Adam's apple stood out?

Elvis Presley, performing at Grand Ole Opry, was fired after one performance and was told to go back to truck driving.

Without a penny, divorced, and raising children on her own, she wrote her first book on an old typewriter. The manuscript was rejected twelve times. Then one publisher agreed to publish the manuscript, but told the author to find a job as 'there was no money in children's books'. Her series of books about Harry Potter sold in millions and she is now one of the richest women in the UK. J.K. Rowling.

When he was 65, he received his first Social Security cheque. When he saw it, he knew that this amount of money would not be able to support him. So he decided to take his life into his own hands. At 65! He had this chicken recipe which was really good, so he went trying to sell the recipe. Nobody wanted it. Then, he started offering people that they wouldn't have to buy his recipe, they would just pay a percentage of their revenue from the chicken they sold. Still nothing. He spend one year travelling around the country and sleeping in his car! And he only had one suit. It took him thousands of rejections and a year spent in his car before he sold his recipe. This man was Colonel Sanders. Now every country in the world has hundreds or even thousands of KFC restaurants.

All because of a dream Colonel Sanders had and strongly believed in it.

He didn't speak until the age of four. He couldn't read until he was seven. His fathers thought he was handicapped. He was expelled from school because later in his school years he would ask teachers questions they couldn't answer! When he went looking for a job, he couldn't find one for more than a year. Years later he won the Nobel Prize and became the most well known physicist in the world. His name? Albert Einstein.

He didn't even make it to his high school's basketball team. He missed over 9,000 shots in his career and lost almost 300 games. And despite all his 'failures', he became the greatest basketball player in history. Michael Jordan.

He was fired from working in a newspaper because his boss told him that he "lacked imagination and had no good ideas". Walt Disney.

He was born in a backwoods cabin.
He had little formal education.
He was a shopkeeper, a postmaster.
In 1832 he lost his job and ran unsuccessfully for state legislature.
In 1834 his business failed.
In 1835 his sweetheart died.
In 1836 he suffered a nervous breakdown.
In 1843 he ran unsuccessfully for Congress.
In 1848 he didn't even get nominated for Congress.
In 1854 he ran unsuccessfully for Senate.
In 1856 he had no success of becoming a Vice President.
In 1860 he became 16th President of the United States.
Abraham Lincoln.

He was told by his teacher that he was hopeless as a composer. Beethoven.

The story of one man touched me profoundly and I want to share it with you.

He used to do quite well, unfortunately he managed to loose everything in a short time. He would spend his days hungry and cold, wandering around the neighbourhood, drinking cheap wine. One day he wanted to end it, he decided he would end his life.

He wanted to end up his miserable life. Never again he wanted to face his life in a mirror. He thought of himself as a failure. He managed to loose everything that was important and precious to him. And on that cold rainy day he was ready to end it all.

Thanks to God he didn't take his life on this cold day in Cleveland. Because if he did, we wouldn't be able to enjoy the amazing, full of life's wisdom books by Og Mandino.

And there is one more. The story of a man who would not quit, that's how strong his dream was. His story has a special meaning for me for one more reason. He was born on exactly the same day as my dad.

From his early years he knew what he wanted to do. He wanted to be in film business. He wanted to inspire people. He wanted to show people that everyone can overcome obstacles no matter how big they are. He wrote his own film and when he started approaching the agents, they all would throw him out saying that the film will not sell and that he would never become a film star. He was thrown out by agents over 1500 times! How many of you would give up after five or ten times?

But he kept going. He was starving. He had no heat in his apartment and his wife would yell at him to get a job. But he didn't want a job because he knew that if he got a job, he would get comfortable in it and would stop pursuing his dream. Isn't it something that so many of us are doing in our lives?

When finally someone liked the script and wanted to buy it, they offered him $125,000 for it (this was in the '70s). But wait. He had one condition. He had to star in it. They said 'no way' and you know what? He left.

Imagine a person with no money and no food walking away from $125,000.

Would you have such a strong believe in your dream that you would walk away because this wasn't the way you wanted it to be?

Some time later, they called him and offered him $250,000 for his film if he wouldn't star in it! Can you believe that? And you know what? He turned it down. That's how strong he believed in his dream.

You may already know who I'm talking about here. Sylvester Stallone's 'Rocky' made $200 million and became a legend.

I want to share one more success story with you. This one is a story of a certain British person who fortunately, for all of us as much as for himself, never gave up on his dreams. You all know him, I'm sure, and this is his story:

The story of the man who never gave up on his dreams.

He was born in a middle-class family and suffered terribly as a child because of his stuttering. He was also teased and bullied at school because of his looks. His bullies thought he looked like an alien. He was soon marked a strange and became a very shy, withdrawn kid who didn't have many friends, so he dived into science.

One of his teachers said: "There was nothing outstanding about him. I did not expect him to be a brilliant scientist, but he has proved everyone wrong."

Admitted to Oxford University during his days, he started falling in love with acting but couldn't perform due to his speaking disorder. He got his master's degree in electrical engineering before appearing in any movie or TV show. After getting his degree, he decided to pursue his dream and become an actor so he enrolled in a comedy group but again, his stammering got in the way.

A lot of TV shows rejected him, and he felt devastated but despite the many rejections. He never stopped believing in himself. He had a great passion for making people laugh and knew that he was very good at it. He started focusing more and more on his original comedy sketches and soon realized that he could speak fluently whenever he played some character. He found a way to overcome his stuttering and this also was used there as an inspiration for his acting. While studying for his master's he co-created the strange, surreal, and now speaking character known as Mr. Bean.

He had success with other shows, Mr. Bean made him globally famous and despite all the obstacles, he faced because of his looks and his speaking disorder, he proved that even without a heroic body or a Hollywood face, you can become one of the most loved and respected actors in the world.

The motivational success story of Rowan Atkinson. It's so inspiring because it teaches us that to be successful in life, the most important things are passion, hard work, dedication and never giving up.

Moral of the story:
No one is born perfect. Don't be afraid. People can accomplish amazing things every day in spite of their weaknesses and failures. So go and do the best you can with the one life you've got.

All of those people who work hard on their dreams, all people who are struggling but believe in brighter future and keep on going even when they don't see results, like yourself. Stick around for a little bit longer. You never know. Success may be just around the corner.

Happiness

> *"Happiness cannot be travelled to,*
> *owned, earned, worn or consumed.*
> *Happiness is the spiritual experience*
> *of living every minute*
> *with love, grace, and gratitude. "*

I have been to many places, I have been to many countries, in so called 'western' world as well as 'eastern' world. Eastern civilisations have always been more like home to me. Here there were people who did not have much and living with little and without comforts. I clearly remember spending time in Siberia in Russia. This was one of my most memorable trips, a trip of a lifetime you could say. At least for now...

We stayed among people who had little by the western standards, and yet there was so much friendliness and they were so happy with the little they had. One could notice that they were happy from within. Happiness, to them, had nothing to do with the latest things one wants to possess. I realised that happiness is something deeper inside. It is something that doesn't depend on circumstances from your external world. It is something deep within you.

Maybe you picked up this book because you're

looking for that 'something' that your life is lacking at the moment. Maybe you picked it up because you want to find out how to take your happiness to the next level. Or maybe you picked it up because you are unhappy and are looking for some answers.

My guess is that somewhere deep inside you you feel that there is more to life than just work, that you deserve to be happy. Hopefully you also feel that life is meant to be abundant and that everyone deserves to be happy and can be happy. And let's get it straight - happiness doesn't depend on external circumstances. When you're happy, really happy, you are unconditionally happy.

To quote 13th century poet, Rumi:

"Happy, not from anything that happens. "

Happiness doesn't have anything to do with money. Despite what media want us to believe, all these "shiny things" will not make us any more happy.

According to recent researches, almost half of the wealthiest people in America are not even as happy as an average American. We are just being seduced to believe that money will buy us happiness. Many people believe it. The reality is you can be happy right here right now if you decide so. You can experience happiness in this very moment. Happiness exists now, not tomorrow or next week. Be in the moment now. And decide to be happy now.

Scientists have proven that everything in our universe is energy. Even you are energy. Everything around you is energy. And the energy either increases or decreases. When your energy increases, you experience happiness and joy. When your energy decreases, you experience less happiness or joy, or no joy at all.

Feeling happy is a habit, and so is feeling like a victim. Many people in our society feel like victims in their lives. They blame everyone else for everything. They blame circumstances for what is happening to them.

However, no matter where you are in your life, it is never too late to change. It is always possible to change your habits.

Think for a moment about time when something happened and you started pondering on the challenge (I like using the word challenge instead of the word problem). If you are like most people, you focused your entire energy on the challenge, possibly even complained about the situation, possibly to other people as well. Does it sound familiar? What if you took all this energy that you spent focusing on complaining or going over the challenge over and over again, and used it to solve the challenge? As I've heard Tony Robbins and many other great people say, you should only spend about 20% of the time and energy on the challenge and spend 80% on finding the solution. Focusing on the solution will give you increase of energy and feeling of happiness, where complaining will only give you less energy and feeling empty. Be a victor, not a victim!

Happiness should be one of your life's goals. You should pursue happiness. After all, nobody wants to be unhappy all their life, right?

Unfortunately not many people pursue happiness. To most people happiness is something that happens because something in their lives happens, like winning or getting a promotion at work.

Instead why not look for opportunities to enjoy happiness? You can enjoy happiness right here right now. You don't need to wait for anything to happen.

Negative Thoughts

*"There is only one cause of unhappiness;
The false beliefs you have in your head,
beliefs so widespread, so commonly held,
that it never occurs to you
to question them."*

Do you have any negative thoughts during the day? Of course you do. Each of us does. This happens to all of us. But you know what? Most of us are ruled by negative thoughts, I'm afraid. For most of us are ruled by the mind instead of ruling the mind. And when you let your mind run these negative thoughts, it's very hard to stay happy. Negative thoughts are killers of our happiness, which is our birthright.

According to scientists, we have about 60,000 thoughts a day, and for most of us 80% of these thoughts are negative and repetitive (they are the same thoughts you had yesterday and the day before yesterday).

Scientists have proven that our thoughts have profound effect on us. It has been proven that when you have negative thoughts, they stimulate the areas of the brain that are involved in depression. Negative thoughts are like poison.

There was an interesting study done at the University of Chicago, which measured electrical activity in the brain. Every person in the study was shown three groups of images: images that created positive, negative, and neutral feelings. As the study has shown, when people were having negative feelings the electrical activity in the brain was at its highest, which caused great impression on the mind. This also has impact on your health. Negative feelings producing high levels of adrenaline have negative impact on your health. The stress chemicals release into the body and accumulate, thus creating disease in the body.

Can you do anything about it? Of course, you can. Your brain is an amazing organ in your body, it can be rewired. Thinking good, positive thoughts will change your brain. Changing thinking produces changes in your brain. As it has been proven by scientists, changing thinking produces new neural pathways. To take it even one step further, a biologist Bruce Lipton suggests through his researches that even our DNA is influenced by our thoughts - negative ones and positive ones alike.

My suggestion to you is - start rewiring your brain with positive thoughts. Decide what your thoughts are going to be like, decide that from now on you're going to think positive thoughts as often as you can. Decide to focus on positive in every situation.

Researches by leading world experts on brain waves show us that brain wave activity for positive and negative people is different. People with positive thinking show more activity in the left pre frontal area of the brain - in the neocortex. People with negative thinking show more activity in the right pre frontal area of the brain. But you know what the great news is? You can change it! How? By practising conscious positive thoughts, by training your mind to focus on the positive instead of the negative.

If I could give you a piece of advice, it would be to shift your energy towards thoughts that serve you. Give positive thoughts more attention, set your focus on positive energy. The more positive thoughts you start thinking the more of the positive thoughts you will attract into your life. Like attracts like. As you start on your quest for happy, positive thoughts, you will start noticing more of the little, positive things in your life. And it's not that they weren't happening to you earlier, you just weren't noticing them.

Do you like playing games? Make it into a game. Stop for a moment. Notice anything positive around you. Use all your senses. Can you see or hear or smell anything beautiful? I'm sure you can come up with something if you try a little harder. As you intentionally, consciously start noticing positive things around you, this will activate you reticular activating system. I remember when I heard about it for the first time from Tony Robbins. Your reticular activating system is responsible for sorting the information coming into your brain and bringing anything it thinks is important to your attention. That's why once you focus on something like a particular car you start noticing it everywhere you go.

If you start practising focusing on positive thoughts and positive feelings, you'll bring more of these into your life. And your life will never be the same...

Happy Body Happy Soul

*"The soul always knows
what to do to heal itself.
The challenge is
to silence the mind. "*

Being happy is not just about thinking happy thoughts, although it helps. Being happy is also about having a happy body, a body in happy state. Your brain is a source of "happiness drugs" as one could call them. These "happiness drugs" are endorphins, dopamine, and serotonin among many others.

Endorphins are our brain's natural painkillers, stronger than morphine (I think I had read somewhere that endorphins are three times(!) stronger than morphine). Incredible.

Dopamine is another brain's drug, which creates a feeling of joy.

Serotonin is responsible for relieving depression and calming the body.

All of our "happiness drugs" are at our disposal all the time and are waiting for us to utilise them. However, most of us are in such hurry all the time and are so stressed that we don't have energy to release our happiness. So many of us are in constant stress and stress has been related to almost all diseases. Then there comes food. We eat in a hurry and we eat very unhealthy foods, processed foods and fast foods.

Stop Complaining

> *"Do not listen to those
> who weep and complain,
> for their disease is contagious."*

What is complaining? It is talking about things you don't want in your life. It is using your language focusing on things that are not the way you would want them to be. Your language, your vocabulary, is the reflection of your thoughts. And your thoughts are the reflection of what you focus on in your life.

You create your life, whether you like it or not, whether you are consciously aware of that or not. You create your life using the thoughts you think all the time. If you don't believe in that, here's a quote for you - from the Bible:

> *"As thou hast believed,
> so be it done unto thee."*
>
> *Matthew 8:13*

Or maybe if you don't believe in Bible and are more of a scientific mind, here's another quote for you:

> *"The highest possible stage in moral culture*
> *is when we recognize that*
> *we ought to control our thoughts."*

It is very important that you control your mind instead of your mind controlling you. I know that most people think of themselves as positive people. People don't think of themselves as negative people. They just think negative thoughts. A lot.

Many people in our world today, way too many, focus on what is wrong with the world instead of focusing on the good side of it. Most of us are unaware of how much of influence has our complaining on our lives. We just think that complaining about the weather or our work is something normal, something that is a part of our lives and we just do it and always have been. It is often hard for us to even realise that we are complaining. It is easier to notice someone else complaining than catch ourselves doing it.

Many people complain to get certain reactions from others, like approval or sympathy. Some people may complain about their health to get sympathy of others. Some people may complain to get noticed.

If you are a person that complains a lot, about your health for example, I need to warn you. Complaining about your health is convincing your body that something's wrong with it even when everything is fine. Your body is then listening to what it is hearing from your mind and is directing energy to attract more of it. That's why sick people are getting sicker as they're complaining about their health. The more you complain about something the more you will have to complain about.

As you are complaining you are affecting not only your own body and mind but also the world around you. We are human beings surrounded by our own energy that cooperates with the energy of people around us. We are all energy beings in human bodies.

Have you ever noticed how when people gather, as one person starts complaining others join this person in complaining? Sometimes a conversation may start with something positive, but as soon as one person starts complaining it becomes like a race. People start trying to convince the rest how bad their lives are. It becomes a contest. A contest of who has the worst life.

This reminds me a scene from one of the shows by the Monthy Python's Flying Circus in which four men try to convince one another who has had the worst life. As you are watching it you know that this is just a show, but if you remember situations like this one from your own life, you start thinking that maybe it's like trying to win in complaining.

I know that bad things happen to us. It happens to all of us. But this doesn't have to push you to complaining. Don't let bad things to be an excuse for complaining and ruining your life. If you look at lives of successful people, they had their challenges and they took them as lessons, and instead of complaining they moved on. They weren't telling everyone around how bad their life was. Instead they looked for good things in their lives and they found them. If you search for something, you will find it.

Sometimes people complain because they feel insecure about something in their lives, i.e. a job. They complain because they feel angry about their situation, even fearful about it.

You need to understand that you cannot control everything that is going on in your life. And complaining about it won't help. If you start complaining less about your situation, you will find that you will worry about it less. Let go off the fear, let go off the worry. Instead, start enjoying your life. Become a more relaxed person, a person who enjoys life instead of complaining about it all the time.

Change your words and you will start changing the world. Start by changing your thoughts first as your thoughts will alter your words. Stop complaining and your mind will start looking for positive thoughts as the negative thoughts will be removed from your thinking. Your mind is always creating feelings and words that come from your thoughts. If you stop complaining and stop thinking negative thoughts, your mind will be filled with the positive ones.

Your Emotions And You

*"The best and most beautiful
things in the world
cannot be seen or even touched.
They must be felt with the heart."*

Have you ever had a feeling of not having something? Or maybe of not having enough of something? Something that you felt missing from your life? Of course you have. We all have. Have you noticed that in that moment you felt a strong desire for that thing? Maybe even the desire was so much stronger when you were feeling lack of it. When you lack something you get a stronger indication of what is missing in your life. And as your desire increases, if it does as so many of us so often dismiss the desire as something unachievable, you will start coming up with ideas and solutions. But you know what? So many of us don't listen to our 'inner voice'. So many of us lost touch with our feelings and don't listen to this voice inside telling us which path to take and how to reach our higher potential. But when you do, you will feel that inner nudge for doing 'the thing', you will feel the clarity of your mind.

Emotions are your compass in life. Emotions tell

you whether you are on track, whether your actions match your inner self. Unfortunately so many of us lost connection with our feelings and emotions so long ago that we find it very hard to get it back. Once you find this connection again, you will feel wonderful.

Your emotions, your emotional inner guidance is all about yourself. Remember that. It is not about other people nor about what other people do or say. Most conflicts between people are caused by others behaving not the way we want them to behave. Often people say: "It's all because he/she doesn't want to change." But ask yourself: "Would you really want him/her to change? Would you want them be what you want them to be?" This doesn't lead anywhere. At least not in the long run. This is not a solution.

Fear And Joy

Worries eat you up when you're alive."
Yiddish proverb

Many people believe that it is their duty to let us know how miserable we are. They seem to love doing it, they seem to love destroying our happiness and our joy in life. Anger they are directing at us is really the anger and rage they have within them. They feel so miserable that they try to pass it onto you.

Have you ever tried to understand why so often we are not full of joy, instead we are full of fear and misery? How is that we 'prefer' to focus on the bad things - things that often bring tears, instead of focusing on the good things - things that bring joy and smile to your face? Some of the answers I often hear are:

" I have to think about serious things like job and money. I'm not a child anymore. " or

" How can I be happy now when the economy is so bad. "

Fear is one of the most common reasons for not being happy. Fear of losing a job, fear of losing a home, or fear of losing a spouse or a significant other. And as you dig deep into your fear, you will get more of it. What you focus on expands. What you focus on, you get more of it. What are some other reasons why we worry?

We worry we are not good enough.

We worry we are not smart enough.

We worry we are not strong enough (not just physically).

We worry that we are going to fail at something we haven't even started yet (and this keeps us from doing the thing we want to do).

We worry that someone will laugh at us when we do what we want to do.

We worry that we won't be loved by someone so we don't even try.

We use our worries to protect ourselves from doing things, we use our worries to protect ourselves from coming out from our comfort zones. Unfortunately, when you don't come out from your comfort zone, you don't grow. And, as we keep worrying about things and situations, we start feeling that we cannot be happy. Worry stops us from doing things, from expanding, from growing. And you know what? Most people fall into this trap. Yes, it is a trap. A trap that keeps you a prisoner within your own life. A trap that holds you entrapped without you even realising it in most cases.

Worrying keeps you focused on negative things, it keeps you away from positive thinking. Your mind cannot be joyful and worried at the same time. At least not for longer period of time.

Fear and worry have negative impact on your body as well. When you think negative thoughts your body is sending signals that have impact on your whole body and change the chemistry of your body. Your brain releases chemicals like adrenaline which affect our bodies and if your body keeps releasing them for longer periods of time, your body starts getting worse. You know that stress caused by fear and worry is causing many illnesses in people's lives. High blood pressure, heart disease, and many others just to mention a few.

Fear and worry, like other feelings we experience, can become addictions. Have you noticed people complaining all the time? Maybe even someone close to you? Have you noticed people who keep focusing on the negative all the time? Feelings can become addictive like smoking or alcohol or drugs. People get so used to it that they can't stop worrying about things. People start reaching for some things trying to deal with worry, or shall I say trying to forget about it. Things like new cars or clothes or electronics like a new phone or a new tablet. Some people reach for food to forget about their worries for a moment. These people get so caught up by the moment that they get addicted to food (and hardly anyone reaches for health food like fruit and vegetables), which makes things even worse.

Here's something I find amazingly interesting. The word 'worry' comes from Latin 'wyrgan', which means 'to strangle'. I even checked the meaning of the word strangle in the dictionary and I found an explanation that fits here perfectly. The Oxford English Dictionary explains 'to strangle' as:

" to supress (a movement or impulse). "

And that's what we do. We suppress our feelings,

our creativity, our potential, our belief in ourselves and in what we could achieve in life.

On the other side we have the word 'joy' which comes from Latin word for 'jewel'. And you know what? You are a jewel. A living jewel. A jewel that can achieve so much in life. A jewel that can (and should) shine like a real jewel.
Remember to live with joy. Be a living jewel.

So what is joy, you may ask? Joy is expressing yourself without judgment, it is creating life on your terms and not someone else's. When you are joyful, you can't feel anger, fear, or insecurity. You just feel joy, joy of being. When you feel joy, you feel at peace with yourself, you feel complete and fulfilled. When you feel joy, every moment of your life feels precious and you want to live it to the fullest. When you feel joy, you are a loving person, you have a loving heart. What is a loving person, a loving heart? Let me explain with this quote from Anthony de Mello:

"What is a loving heart?
A loving heart is sensitive to the whole of life,
to all persons;
a loving heart doesn't harden itself
to any person or thing. "

Many believe that joy is reserved for few when in reality joy is for everyone to experience. We live in times that lack joy, times of joyless lives of so many people. For many joy is hard to describe, hard to express. Many find it easier to talk about things like anxiety and fear of everyday life instead of joy.

Think for a moment about a time when you were sick or your body was hurting. Did you talk about it to people around you? Did you express your anxiety about the pain you were experiencing? How about moments when you were feeling well and you were happy/joyful? Where you talking to people around you about the joy you were experiencing? Probably not.

Does it mean that our lives have less joy and more sad times? Or does it mean that we just prefer talking about sad, less joyful experiences? Maybe our feelings of joy are just harder to express. Maybe it is hard to find words to express our joy.

When it comes to fear, it makes joy impossible to experience. And what is sad is that so often the fear is not real. So often we feel fear for something that doesn't come. As someone once beautifully explained the word fear:

False
Evidence
Appearing
Real.

The real joy is the joy that you feel every day. It is a joy that stays with you in good health and in sickness, in good times and bad times, no matter what happens in the world. Your joy is the celebration of life. Real joy is joy that cannot be given to you by someone else and nor can it be taken away from you, unless you give it away. Your joy should be so strong that nothing will be able to destroy it.

Joy Of Giving

*"You give but little
when you give of your possessions.
It is when you give of yourself
that you truly give."*

The joy of giving is a true meaning of success. Any success. There is so much you can learn from this amazing act of giving.

Giving is a powerful act. Giving, without expecting anything in exchange, will draw abundance into your life as a giver. No doubt about that. When you give unconditionally and unselfishly, without expecting anything in exchange, it creates a magnetic force and affects your life. It also gives you an amazing feeling of fulfilment. You grow mentally, physically and spiritually.

The universal laws are controlled by the acts of giving and receiving.

From the spiritual point of view, you will be rewarded when the time is right or in other words taken from the book of Galatians "you will harvest what you sow".

From the scientific point of view, in the words of one of the greatest British scientists - Isaac Newton,

"for each action there is an equal reaction".

Whichever way you look at things, these universal laws are incorporated into everyone's daily life, and sooner or later you will attract and create an abundance and success that you desire. This is the act of giving in action.

Most people see giving as related to money but it is not just about money. The real true meaning of giving goes far beyond just giving money. It is true that most donating is in the terms of money but the amount we give, either in monetary terms or otherwise, does not measure our real worth.

Giving, giving from the heart in a selfless act, is a very empowering experience and a very rewarding one. It is an act that is not connected to any special occasion or any special day. It is rather an act of compassion. It is an act of giving unconditionally to show gratitude for what you have and to show that you care about other people. And especially, when you don't expect anything in return.

Action

*"You don't have to be great to start,
but you do have to start to be great."*

The world doesn't remember for how much you know. The world remembers for what you have done.

So many people don't achieve success in their lives because they don't know how to get things done.

As Bob Proctor said:

*"The biggest handicap to a person's success
is not a lack of brains,
nor a lack of character or willingness
- it is in their inability to get things done."*

All these people know that they have things to do. They know how to get these things done. But they never do that. They keep procrastinating, postponing things and never do them. Their days lack meaning. They're often people looking forward to the weekend and counting the days during the week welcoming Saturday with open arms. And as they're looking forward to the weekend they never really live the weekdays.

They don't get anywhere as they don't have a specific plan how to achieve what they're trying to achieve. Sometimes they work hard. But they don't work effectively. They look at things instead of starting them. They put things off day by day and they never start. Or if they do start they never finish what they started. They don't plan so they don't know what they're supposed to do.

The Story of David

> *"The Lord is my strength and my shield;*
> *my heart trusted in him, and I am helped;*
> *therefore my heart greatly rejoiceth;*
> *and with my song will I praise him."*

Are you familiar with the story of David from the Old Testament? If not, let me tell you a little bit about David before I tell you the most interest story about his life.

David was born in Bethlehem, in the land of Judah. David was the courageous boy who slew the Goliath, and who, on presenting Goliath's head to the king Saul became a national hero. King Saul selected David to be a warrior in his army. David's successes became so great that the verse says:

> *"When the [troops] came home [and] David*
> *returned from killing the Philistines,*
> *the women of all the towns of Israel came out . . .*
> *The women sang as they danced, and they chanted:*
> *'Saul has slain his thousands;*
> *David, his tens of thousands!'"*

And here's the most interesting part:

There was a prophet called Samuel, who was told by God that he would find the future King in the home of Jesse. Jesse had many sons and one of them was going to become the King.

Jesse, hesitating, mentioned that he had one more son but as he said "he was only a shepherd" and was right now attending to the livestock.

Samuel asked Jesse to bring his last son and when the youngest son arrives, Samuel says to Jesse:

"This is the King."

There is a powerful messages in this story. Even his own father didn't recognise the future King in his own son. His father couldn't see what was inside of him. He also couldn't believe that David could be the future King. And his brothers probably didn't want to believe it.

Next, Samuel said something very powerful to Jesse:

"Man looks on the outside, God looks on the inside."

Why am I telling you this story? Because it doesn't matter where you are right now. It doesn't matter whether you are too tall, too short, too white, too black, or whether you're broke right now. Or whether you're too young or too old. Because no matter what is happening with you right now, no matter what you look on the outside, you have the power to change your life. You have the power to become a great person. You have the power to accomplish something, to do something with your life.

You need to realise that there is a power inside you, sleeping and waiting to be awakened. And do not allow anyone to tell you that you cannot do something or cannot achieve something.

There is one more powerful story that involves king David, where the tradition says the story of Adam who was going to live 1,000 years but he didn't. There is this story where Adam asked God to show him the future, to which God agreed. God took Adam on a journey through different rooms where there were flames burning for the souls that were going to be born. Each soul had a flame, some flames were burning just a little bit where others would burn a lot.

At some point, Adam saw a beautiful flame, probably one of the most beautiful he saw in this place. So he asked God that this is probably going to be an amazing person born and he asked when this soul is going to be born.

God replied: "I'm sorry, Adam, but that soul, as beautiful as it is, is destined not to be born. It has been preordained that it will commit sin and tarnish itself. I have chosen to spare it indignity to be dishonoured."

Adam started pleading with God, asking him to let this soul live, but God said that the decision had been made and that he had no more years left to allocate to this soul.

So, Adam pleaded with God to allow this soul to live and he, Adam, would give some of his years of his life for this soul to live. To that, God agreed if that was Adam's wish.

As we know from the Bible, Adam did not get to live 1,000 years. He lived for 930 years. As you can guess by now, Adam gave 70 years of his life to this soul so that it could live.

What was this soul, you may be asking?

Some years later, a child was born in Bethlehem. This child became an Israel ruler and a singer of beautiful songs. He would lead his people.

And the Bible says: "Behold, David the King was buried after having lived for 70 years."

Prologue

> *"What is life?*
> *Life is a collection of moments.*
> *Cherish them because they will never come back.*
> *Each moment and each experience happens once.*
> *Past is gone*
> *and tomorrow hasn't happened yet.*
> *There is only Now.*
> *Cherish this very moment.*
> *Carpe diem. "*
>
> *Marek Mularczyk*

We come to the end of our journey together. Thank you for joining me on this journey. Remember that life is a journey and what matters most is not the destination but the life itself.

Live your life with passion. Live your life as if today was your last day on earth. Life is too short and too beautiful to be left for living later. Do it now. Do not hesitate.

Life goes so quickly. I believe that when we are born someone should tell us straight away that right from the beginning we start dying and we should start living straight away and not waste our precious time that we have right here right now.

Why have I written this book? Out of desire to try to help you. If this book helps you in any way, it will give me happiness.

We may never meet. However, in a way, we have met through this book.

I wish you all the happiness and God bless you.

Marek

P.S. I want to share with you a beautiful short poem, which hopefully will help you when the times are hard, to uplift you, to help you express gratitude for what you have and to give you hope.

It's called "Oh God, forgive me when I whine":

Oh God, forgive me when I whine

*Today, upon a bus, I saw a girl with golden hair.
I envied her, she seemed to gay, and I wished I was as fair.
When suddenly she rose to leave,
I saw her hobbled down the aisle.
She had one leg and wore a crutch.
And as she passed…. A smile.*

*Oh God, forgive me when I whine.
I have 2 legs, the world is mine.*

*I stopped to buy some candy.
The lad who sold it had such charm.
I talked with him, he seemed so glad.
If I were late, it'd do no harm.
And as I left, he said to me,
"I thank you, you've been so kind.
It's nice to talk with folks like you.
You see," he said, "I'm blind."*

*Oh God, forgive me when I whine.
I have 2 eyes, the world is mine.*

continues on the next page

Later while walking down the street,
I saw a child with eyes of blue.
He stood and watched the others play.
He did not know what to do.
I stopped for a moment and then I said,
"Why don't you join the others, dear?"

He looked ahead without a word.
And then I knew, he couldn't hear.

Oh God, forgive me when I whine.
I have 2 ears, the world is mine.

With feet to take me where I'd go.
With eyes to see the sunset's glow.
With ears to hear what I'd known.

Oh God, forgive me when I whine.
I've been blessed indeed, the world is mine....

Contents

Introduction	11
A New Chapter in Life	17
Pursuit of Happiness	23
Change Your Life	25
Be an optimist.	31
Make mistakes.	33
Find a Hobby	35
Thank Someone	37
Your Health	39
Challenges	41
Success	45
Wins And Failures	47
Happiness	57
Negative Thoughts	61
Happy Body Happy Soul	65
Stop Complaining	67
Your Emotions And You	71
Fear And Joy	73
Joy Of Giving	79
Action	81
The Story of David	83
Prologue	87

www.ingramcontent.com/pod-product-compliance
Lightning Source LLC
Chambersburg PA
CBHW062103290426
44110CB00022B/2696